Sentences for Consonant Blends & Digraphs

Author . . . . Marsha Elyn Wright
Editor . . . . Kathy Rogers
Cover Design . . . . Ken Tunell

Table of Contents

Introduction 2

Consonant Blends—Initial
bl– 3
br– 4
Review bl– and br– 5
cl– 6
cr– 7
Review cl– and cr– 8
fl– 9
fr– 10
Review fl– and fr– 11
gl– 12
gr– 13
Review gl– and gr– 14
pl– 15
pr– 16
Review pl– and pr– 17
sl– 18
sm– 19
Review sl– and sm– 20
sk– 21
sn– 22
sp– 23
Review sk–, sn–, and sp– 24
st– 25
sw– 26
tr– 27

Review st–, sw–, and tr– 28

Consonant Blends—Final
–ft 29
–nd 30
–ng 31
Review –ft, –nd, and –ng 32
–nk 33
–nt 34
–st 35
Review –nk, –nt, and –st 36

Consonant Digraphs—Initial
ch– 37
kn– 38
sh– 39
Review ch–, kn– and sh– 40
th– (then) 41
th– (thin) 42
wh– 43
Review th– and wh– 44

Consonant Digraphs—Final
–ch 45
–ck 46
–sh 47
Review –ch, –ck, and –sh 48

Reproducible for classroom use only.
Not for use by an entire school or school system.
EP193 • ©2003 Edupress, Inc.™ • P.O. Box 883 • Dana Point, CA 92629
www.edupressinc.com
ISBN 1-56472-193-0
Printed in USA

Introduction

Teachers know that phonics is an important part of literacy instruction. By introducing children to phonetically spelled words and word families, they begin to recognize familiar spelling patterns. They learn to decode by analogy. They develop a store of instant words and learn how to use patterns in familiar words to decode and spell hundreds of unfamiliar words. With this approach to phonics, children become better readers.

Teachers also know that writing is the other necessary part of literacy instruction. As children become better readers, they become better writers! *Sentences for Consonant Blends & Digraphs* uses a phonics-based writing approach to build better readers and writers. Every page provides students with the following:

- **Word Bank based on phonetically regular words**
- **Lines on which students write four words from the Word Bank**
- **Space for student illustrations**
- **Sentence frame for students to complete**
- **Lines for students to copy a sentence or write a sentence of their own**

The activity pages can be used in a variety of ways:

- **Introduce (or review) a specific phonics skill or word family**—List the individual words on the board and discuss each word and its meaning. Have each student choose four words from the Word Bank and draw a picture of each within the boxes provided. Then have students write each word under its picture. Instruct students to copy the first sentence given. Have students complete the second sentence by using one or more words from the Word Bank. Then have each student use words from the Word Bank to write an original sentence.

- **Use as a resource for your classroom Word Wall**—Use a thick marker to write the words from the Word Bank on separate sheets of colored paper (large enough to be seen from anyplace in the classroom). Cut around the outline of the letters to create a visual image of each word. Post these colorful words in their appropriate places on your Word Wall.

- **Assign independently as homework.**

- **Compile into student-made books for your classroom.**

In this phonics-based writing series, use the companion book—*Stories for Consonant Blends & Digraphs*—to reinforce the words provided in each Word Bank.

bl-

1. Choose four words from the word bank.
2. Draw pictures of the words in the boxes.
3. Write the word under each picture.

Name _____

Word Bank

black   block
Blair   blond
blank   blow
blew   blue
blimp   bluff
blind   blush

1. Copy the sentence.
2. Use words from the word bank to finish the sentence.
3. Use words from the word bank to write your own sentence.

1. The blimp blew away.

2. The block is

3.

Sentences for Consonant Blends & Digraphs   3   ©EDUPRESS, INC.™   EP193

br–

1. Choose four words from the word bank.
2. Draw pictures of the words in the boxes.
3. Write the word under each picture.

Name_____

Word Bank

Brad bring
brag brook
brand broom
brat broth
brick brown
brim brush

1. Copy the sentence.
2. Use words from the word bank to finish the sentence.
3. Use words from the word bank to write your own sentence.

1. Brad has a brush.

2. Bring me the

3.

Sentences for Consonant Blends & Digraphs   4   ©EDUPRESS, INC.™   EP193

Review bl-/br-

1. Choose four words from the word bank.
2. Draw pictures of the words in the boxes.
3. Write the word under each picture.

Name_____

Word Bank

black	brag
Blair	brick
blank	bring
blimp	broom
block	brown
blond	brush

1. Copy the sentence.
2. Use words from the word bank to finish the sentence.
3. Use words from the word bank to write your own sentence.

1. I see a black blimp.

2. I see a brown

3.

Sentences for Consonant Blends & Digraphs   ©EDUPRESS, INC.™   EP193

cl-

1. Choose four words from the word bank.
2. Draw pictures of the words in the boxes.
3. Write the word under each picture.

Name _____

Word Bank

clam   climb
clap   cling
class   clock
claw   close
clay   cloud
cliff   club

1. Copy the sentence.
2. Use words from the word bank to finish the sentence.
3. Use words from the word bank to write your own sentence.

1. I made a clay clam.

2. I can climb the

3.

Sentences for Consonant Blends & Digraphs   6   ©EDUPRESS, INC.™   EP193

cr-

1. Choose four words from the word bank.
2. Draw pictures of the words in the boxes.
3. Write the word under each picture.

Name_____

Word Bank

crab   crib
crack   croak
cramp   crop
crane   cross
crash   crow
crawl   cry

1. Copy the sentence.
2. Use words from the word bank to finish the sentence.
3. Use words from the word bank to write your own sentence.

1. The crib has a crack.

2. The crab will

3.

Sentences for Consonant Blends & Digraphs   7   ©EDUPRESS, INC.™   EP193

Review cl-/cr-

1. Choose four words from the word bank.
2. Draw pictures of the words in the boxes.
3. Write the word under each picture.

Name_____

Word Bank

clam   crab
claw   crane
clay   crash
cliff   crawl
climb   croak
cloud   cry

1. Copy the sentence.
2. Use words from the word bank to finish the sentence.
3. Use words from the word bank to write your own sentence.

1. A clam can climb.

2. I see the crab

3.

Sentences for Consonant Blends & Digraphs 8 ©EDUPRESS, INC.™ EP193

fl-

1. Choose four words from the word bank.
2. Draw pictures of the words in the boxes.
3. Write the word under each picture.

Name_____

Word Bank

flag   flick
flap   flip
flash   floor
flat   flop
flea   flow
flew   fly

1. Copy the sentence.
2. Use words from the word bank to finish the sentence.
3. Use words from the word bank to write your own sentence.

1. I did a flip.

2. The fly

3.

Sentences for Consonant Blends & Digraphs   9   ©EDUPRESS, INC.™   EP193

fr-

1. Choose four words from the word bank.
2. Draw pictures of the words in the boxes.
3. Write the word under each picture.

Name_____

Word Bank

Fran   frog
Fred   from
free   front
fresh   frost
friend fruit
frizz   fry

1. Copy the sentence.
2. Use words from the word bank to finish the sentence.
3. Use words from the word bank to write your own sentence.

1. Go to the front.

2. Fran has a

3.

Sentences for Consonant Blends & Digraphs   10   ©EDUPRESS, INC.™   EP193

Review fl-/fr-

1. Choose four words from the word bank.
2. Draw pictures of the words in the boxes.
3. Write the word under each picture.

Name _____

Word Bank

flag   Fred
flap   free
flea   frog
flew   from
flip   front
fly   fry

1. Copy the sentence.
2. Use words from the word bank to finish the sentence.
3. Use words from the word bank to write your own sentence.

1. The flag flew.

2. The frog did a

3.

Sentences for Consonant Blends & Digraphs   11   ©EDUPRESS, INC.™   EP193

gl-

1. Choose four words from the word bank.
2. Draw pictures of the words in the boxes.
3. Write the word under each picture.

Name _____

Word Bank

glad　　Gloria
glare　　glob
glass　　gloom
Glen　　glove
glide　　glow
glider　　glue

1. Copy the sentence.
2. Use words from the word bank to finish the sentence.
3. Use words from the word bank to write your own sentence.

1. I have a glob of glue.

2. Gloria is

3.

Sentences for Consonant Blends & Digraphs　　12　　©EDUPRESS, INC.™　　EP193

gr-

Name _____

1. Choose four words from the word bank.
2. Draw pictures of the words in the boxes.
3. Write the word under each picture.

Word Bank

grab   grew
grand   grill
grass   grim
gray   grin
green   grip
Greg   grow

1. Copy the sentence.
2. Use words from the word bank to finish the sentence.
3. Use words from the word bank to write your own sentence.

1. Grip the gray grill.

2. The grass is

3.

Sentences for Consonant Blends & Digraphs   13   ©EDUPRESS, INC.™   EP193

Review gl-/gr-

1. Choose four words from the word bank.
2. Draw pictures of the words in the boxes.
3. Write the word under each picture.

Name _____

Word Bank

glad   grab
glass   grass
Glen   gray
glide   green
glove   grew
glow   grin

1. Copy the sentence.
2. Use words from the word bank to finish the sentence.
3. Use words from the word bank to write your own sentence.

1. Glen is glad.

2. Grab the green

3.

Sentences for Consonant Blends & Digraphs

pl-

1. Choose four words from the word bank.
2. Draw pictures of the words in the boxes.
3. Write the word under each picture.

Name _____

Word Bank

plan   plop
plank   plow
plant   plug
plate   plum
play   plump
plod   plunk

1. Copy the sentence.
2. Use words from the word bank to finish the sentence.
3. Use words from the word bank to write your own sentence.

1. This is a plum plant.

2. I like to

3.

Sentences for Consonant Blends & Digraphs   15   ©EDUPRESS, INC.™   EP193

pr–

1. Choose four words from the word bank.
2. Draw pictures of the words in the boxes.
3. Write the word under each picture.

Name _____

Word Bank

prank   prince

pray   princess

press   prick

pretty   print

price   prize

pride   prop

1. Copy the sentence.
2. Use words from the word bank to finish the sentence.
3. Use words from the word bank to write your own sentence.

1. The prince has a prize.

2. The princess is

3.

Sentences for Consonant Blends & Digraphs   16   ©EDUPRESS, INC.™   EP193

Review pl-/pr-

1. Choose four words from the word bank.
2. Draw pictures of the words in the boxes.
3. Write the word under each picture.

Name _____

Word Bank

plan   pretty
plant   price
plate   prince
play   princess
plow   print
plum   prize

1. Copy the sentence.
2. Use words from the word bank to finish the sentence.
3. Use words from the word bank to write your own sentence.

1. Plant the plum.

2. The prize is a

3.

Sentences for Consonant Blends & Digraphs   17   ©EDUPRESS, INC.™   EP193

sl–

1. Choose four words from the word bank.
2. Draw pictures of the words in the boxes.
3. Write the word under each picture.

Name _____

Word Bank

slam   slid
slap   slim
sled   slip
sleek   slow
sleep   slug
slick   sly

1. Copy the sentence.
2. Use words from the word bank to finish the sentence.
3. Use words from the word bank to write your own sentence.

1. The slick sled slid.

2. The slim slug is

3.

Sentences for Consonant Blends & Digraphs   18   ©EDUPRESS, INC.™   EP193

sm-

1. Choose four words from the word bank.
2. Draw pictures of the words in the boxes.
3. Write the word under each picture.

Name _____

Word Bank

smack   smile
small   smirk
smart   smock
smash   smog
smear   smoke
smell   smooth

1. Copy the sentence.
2. Use words from the word bank to finish the sentence.
3. Use words from the word bank to write your own sentence.

1. The small boy is smart.

2. I smell

3.

Sentences for Consonant Blends & Digraphs ©EDUPRESS, INC.™ EP193

Review sl-/sm-

1. Choose four words from the word bank.
2. Draw pictures of the words in the boxes.
3. Write the word under each picture.

Name _____

Word Bank

sled   small

sleek   smart

sleep   smash

slid   smell

slow   smog

slug   smooth

1. Copy the sentence.
2. Use words from the word bank to finish the sentence.
3. Use words from the word bank to write your own sentence.

1. The slow slug slid.

2. The sled was

3.

Sentences for Consonant Blends & Digraphs 20 ©EDUPRESS, INC.™ EP193

sk-

1. Choose four words from the word bank.
2. Draw pictures of the words in the boxes.
3. Write the word under each picture.

Name_____

Word Bank

skate   Skip
ski   skirt
skid   skit
skill   skull
skim   skunk
skin   sky

1. Copy the sentence.
2. Use words from the word bank to finish the sentence.
3. Use words from the word bank to write your own sentence.

1. Skip saw a skunk.

2. I like to

3.

Sentences for Consonant Blends & Digraphs   21   ©EDUPRESS, INC.™   EP193

sn-

1. Choose four words from the word bank.
2. Draw pictures of the words in the boxes.
3. Write the word under each picture.

Name _____

Word Bank

snack   sniff

snail   snip

snake   snoop

snap   snort

snarl   snow

sneak   snug

1. Copy the sentence.
2. Use words from the word bank to finish the sentence.
3. Use words from the word bank to write your own sentence.

1. The snake had a snack.

2. The dog gave a

3.

Sentences for Consonant Blends & Digraphs

sp-

1. Choose four words from the word bank.
2. Draw pictures of the words in the boxes.
3. Write the word under each picture.

Name_____

Word Bank

speak   spin
sped   spit
spell   spoke
spend   spoon
spider Spot
spill   spun

1. Copy the sentence.
2. Use words from the word bank to finish the sentence.
3. Use words from the word bank to write your own sentence.

1. The spider spun a web.

2. Do not

3.

Sentences for Consonant Blends & Digraphs   23   ©EDUPRESS, INC.™   EP193

Review sk-/sn-/sp-

1. Choose four words from the word bank.
2. Draw pictures of the words in the boxes.
3. Write the word under each picture.

Name_____

Word Bank

skate	sniff
Skip	snow
skunk	spider
sky	spill
snake	spun
snap	Spot

1. Copy the sentence.
2. Use words from the word bank to finish the sentence.
3. Use words from the word bank to write your own sentence.

1. Snow fell from the sky.

2. Spot is a

3.

Sentences for Consonant Blends & Digraphs 24 ©EDUPRESS, INC.™ EP193

st–

1. Choose four words from the word bank.
2. Draw pictures of the words in the boxes.
3. Write the word under each picture.

Name _____

Word Bank

stall   step
stamp   stick
stand   stiff
star   sting
stay   stop
stem   story

1. Copy the sentence.
2. Use words from the word bank to finish the sentence.
3. Use words from the word bank to write your own sentence.

1. Step and stand here.

2. The stick is

3.

Sentences for Consonant Blends & Digraphs   ©EDUPRESS, INC.™   EP193

sw-

1. Choose four words from the word bank.
2. Draw pictures of the words in the boxes.
3. Write the word under each picture.

Name _____

Word Bank

swab   sway

swam   sweep

swan   sweet

swap   swell

swarm   swim

swat   swing

1. Copy the sentence.
2. Use words from the word bank to finish the sentence.
3. Use words from the word bank to write your own sentence.

1. Don't swing and sway.

2. The swan will

3.

Sentences for Consonant Blends & Digraphs   26   ©EDUPRESS, INC.™   EP193

tr-

1. Choose four words from the word bank.
2. Draw pictures of the words in the boxes.
3. Write the word under each picture.

Name_____

Word Bank

track   trick
train   trim
trap   trip
trash   troll
tray   trot
tree   truck

1. Copy the sentence.
2. Use words from the word bank to finish the sentence.
3. Use words from the word bank to write your own sentence.

1. I see the trash truck.

2. Mom will trim the

3.

Sentences for Consonant Blends & Digraphs   27   ©EDUPRESS, INC.™   EP193

Review st-/sw-/tr-

1. Choose four words from the word bank.
2. Draw pictures of the words in the boxes.
3. Write the word under each picture.

Name _____

Word Bank

stem	swim
stand	swing
star	trap
stick	tree
swan	trip
swat	truck

1. Copy the sentence.
2. Use words from the word bank to finish the sentence.
3. Use words from the word bank to write your own sentence.

1. The truck took a trip.

2. Stand by the

3.

Sentences for Consonant Blends & Digraphs   ©EDUPRESS, INC.™   EP193

–ft

1. Choose four words from the word bank.
2. Draw pictures of the words in the boxes.
3. Write the word under each picture.

Name_____

Word Bank

left   swift
theft   loft
drift   soft
gift   craft
lift   draft
sift   raft

1. Copy the sentence.
2. Use words from the word bank to finish the sentence.
3. Use words from the word bank to write your own sentence.

1. The raft will drift.

2. Lift the

3.

Sentences for Consonant Blends & Digraphs   29   ©EDUPRESS, INC.™   EP193

−nd

1. Choose four words from the word bank.
2. Draw pictures of the words in the boxes.
3. Write the word under each picture.

Name_____

Word Bank

and   end
band   lend
hand   send
land   find
sand   kind
bend   mind

1. Copy the sentence.
2. Use words from the word bank to finish the sentence.
3. Use words from the word bank to write your own sentence.

1. My hand can bend.

2. Find me some

3.

Sentences for Consonant Blends & Digraphs   30   ©EDUPRESS, INC.™   EP193

-ng

1. Choose four words from the word bank.
2. Draw pictures of the words in the boxes.
3. Write the word under each picture.

Name_____

Word Bank

bang   bing
clang   ding
gang   king
hang   ring
rang   sing
sang   wing

1. Copy the sentence.
2. Use words from the word bank to finish the sentence.
3. Use words from the word bank to write your own sentence.

1. The gang sang.

2. The king will

3.

Sentences for Consonant Blends & Digraphs   31   ©EDUPRESS, INC.™   EP193

Review –ft/–nd/–ng

1. Choose four words from the word bank.
2. Draw pictures of the words in the boxes.
3. Write the word under each picture.

Name _____

Word Bank

drift   sand
gift   find
swift   kind
craft   king
raft   ring
land   sing

1. Copy the sentence.
2. Use words from the word bank to finish the sentence.
3. Use words from the word bank to write your own sentence.

1. I will find the king.

2. The raft will

3.

Sentences for Consonant Blends & Digraphs   32   ©EDUPRESS, INC.™   EP193

−nk

1. Choose four words from the word bank.
2. Draw pictures of the words in the boxes.
3. Write the word under each picture.

Name_____

Word Bank

bank   mink
Hank   pink
rank   rink
sank   sink
tank   wink
link   bunk

1. Copy the sentence.
2. Use words from the word bank to finish the sentence.
3. Use words from the word bank to write your own sentence.

1. The tank sank.

2. Mom has a pink

3.

Sentences for Consonant Blends & Digraphs   33   ©EDUPRESS, INC.™   EP193

—nt

1. Choose four words from the word bank.
2. Draw pictures of the words in the boxes.
3. Write the word under each picture.

Name_____

Word Bank

ant   rent
pant   sent
want   tent
bent   went
cent   mint
lent   tint

1. Copy the sentence.
2. Use words from the word bank to finish the sentence.
3. Use words from the word bank to write your own sentence.

1. I lent Dad a cent.

2. He sent me a

3.

Sentences for Consonant Blends & Digraphs   34   ©EDUPRESS, INC.™   EP193

—st

1. Choose four words from the word bank.
2. Draw pictures of the words in the boxes.
3. Write the word under each picture.

Name_____

Word Bank

best   zest

nest   host

pest   most

rest   post

test   just

west   must

1. Copy the sentence.
2. Use words from the word bank to finish the sentence.
3. Use words from the word bank to write your own sentence.

1. Rest by the post.

2. This is the best

3.

Sentences for Consonant Blends & Digraphs   35   ©EDUPRESS, INC.™   EP193

Review -nk/-nt/-st

1. Choose four words from the word bank.
2. Draw pictures of the words in the boxes.
3. Write the word under each picture.

Name _____

Word Bank

Hank   tent
sank   went
pink   best
mink   nest
cent   rest
sent   west

1. Copy the sentence.
2. Use words from the word bank to finish the sentence.
3. Use words from the word bank to write your own sentence.

1. Hank went west.

2. He sent us a

3.

Sentences for Consonant Blends & Digraphs   36   ©EDUPRESS, INC.™   EP193

ch-

1. Choose four words from the word bank.
2. Draw pictures of the words in the boxes.
3. Write the word under each picture.

Name _____

Word Bank

chalk   chick

chase   child

chat   chill

cheek   chin

cheer   chip

chew   chop

1. Copy the sentence.
2. Use words from the word bank to finish the sentence.
3. Use words from the word bank to write your own sentence.

1. The chalk has a chip.

2. The child has a

3.

Sentences for Consonant Blends & Digraphs   37   ©EDUPRESS, INC.™   EP193

kn-

1. Choose four words from the word bank.
2. Draw pictures of the words in the boxes.
3. Write the word under each picture.

Name _____

Word Bank

knack   knit

knee   knob

kneel   knock

knelt   knoll

knew   knot

knife   know

1. Copy the sentence.
2. Use words from the word bank to finish the sentence.
3. Use words from the word bank to write your own sentence.

1. The knife cut the knot.

2. I know how to

3.

Sentences for Consonant Blends & Digraphs   38   ©EDUPRESS, INC.™   EP193

sh-

1. Choose four words from the word bank.
2. Draw pictures of the words in the boxes.
3. Write the word under each picture.

Name_____

Word Bank

shade   shirt
shark   shoe
sheep   shop
shelf   shovel
shell   shut
ship   shy

1. Copy the sentence.
2. Use words from the word bank to finish the sentence.
3. Use words from the word bank to write your own sentence.

1. The shirt is on a shelf.

2. I see a shy

3.

Sentences for Consonant Blends & Digraphs   39   ©EDUPRESS, INC.™   EP193

Review ch-/kn-/sh-

1. Choose four words from the word bank.
2. Draw pictures of the words in the boxes.
3. Write the word under each picture.

Name _____

Word Bank

chair   know

chalk   knock

chick   shark

child   ship

knee   shell

knife   shovel

1. Copy the sentence.
2. Use words from the word bank to finish the sentence.
3. Use words from the word bank to write your own sentence.

1. I know how to shovel.

2. A child sat on a

3.

Sentences for Consonant Blends & Digraphs   40   ©EDUPRESS, INC.™   EP193

th-

1. Choose four words from the word bank.
2. Draw pictures of the words in the boxes.
3. Write the word under each picture.

Name _____

Word Bank

than   there
that   these
the   they
their   this
them   those
then   though

1. Copy the sentence.
2. Use words from the word bank to finish the sentence.
3. Use words from the word bank to write your own sentence.

1. There they go!

2. I see

3.

Sentences for Consonant Blends & Digraphs 41 ©EDUPRESS, INC.™ EP193

th-

1. Choose four words from the word bank.
2. Draw pictures of the words in the boxes.
3. Write the word under each picture.

Name _____

Word Bank

thank   three

thick   threw

thief   thrill

thin   throw

things   thumb

think   thump

1. Copy the sentence.
2. Use words from the word bank to finish the sentence.
3. Use words from the word bank to write your own sentence.

1. A thief made a thump.

2. I think I hurt my

3.

Sentences for Consonant Blends & Digraphs

wh-

1. Choose four words from the word bank.
2. Draw pictures of the words in the boxes.
3. Write the word under each picture.

Name_____

Word Bank

whale   which
what   whiff
wheat   while
wheel   whip
when   white
where   why

1. Copy the sentence.
2. Use words from the word bank to finish the sentence.
3. Use words from the word bank to write your own sentence.

1. Wheel the wheat here.

2. I see a white

3.

Sentences for Consonant Blends & Digraphs   43   ©EDUPRESS, INC.™   EP193

Review th-/wh-

1. Choose four words from the word bank.
2. Draw pictures of the words in the boxes.
3. Write the word under each picture.

Name _____

Word Bank

the   things
their   three
them   thumb
there   wheat
they   wheel
thief   whip

1. Copy the sentence.
2. Use words from the word bank to finish the sentence.
3. Use words from the word bank to write your own sentence.

1. The wheat is for them.

2. A thief took our

3.

Sentences for Consonant Blends & Digraphs   44   ©EDUPRESS, INC.™   EP193

-ch

1. Choose four words from the word bank.
2. Draw pictures of the words in the boxes.
3. Write the word under each picture.

Name _____

Word Bank

beach   catch
each   latch
peach   match
reach   patch
teach   much
batch   such

1. Copy the sentence.
2. Use words from the word bank to finish the sentence.
3. Use words from the word bank to write your own sentence.

1. I see a peach patch.

2. We will go to a

3.

Sentences for Consonant Blends & Digraphs   45   ©EDUPRESS, INC.™   EP193

-ck

1. Choose four words from the word bank.
2. Draw pictures of the words in the boxes.
3. Write the word under each picture.

Name_____

Word Bank

back   pick
Jack   sick
lack   wick
pack   lock
rack   rock
sack   sock

1. Copy the sentence.
2. Use words from the word bank to finish the sentence.
3. Use words from the word bank to write your own sentence.

1. Jack is back.

2. A rock is in my

3.

Sentences for Consonant Blends & Digraphs

–sh

1. Choose four words from the word bank.
2. Draw pictures of the words in the boxes.
3. Write the word under each picture.

Name _____

Word Bank

ash   sash
cash   dish
dash   fish
gash   wish
mash bush
rash   push

1. Copy the sentence.
2. Use words from the word bank to finish the sentence.
3. Use words from the word bank to write your own sentence.

1. Buy the sash with cash.

2. Put the fish on a

3.

Sentences for Consonant Blends & Digraphs   47   ©EDUPRESS, INC.™   EP193

Review -ch/-ck/-sh

1. Choose four words from the word bank.
2. Draw pictures of the words in the boxes.
3. Write the word under each picture.

Name _____

Word Bank

peach   sack
reach   rock
batch   sock
catch   dish
Jack   fish
pack   wish

1. Copy the sentence.
2. Use words from the word bank to finish the sentence.
3. Use words from the word bank to write your own sentence.

1. Jack will pack.

2. I wish for a

3.

Sentences for Consonant Blends & Digraphs   48   ©EDUPRESS, INC.™   EP193